Front cover illustrated by Fleur Davies © Neville Layhe 2022
Instagram - @fleurclariceart

ISBN Number 9798429627533

Published by Amazon.

Dedication

I dedicate this narrative to house-wife, the late Ada Ellen Layhe, and the late William Charles Layhe, Chief Fire Officer at BICC Prescot, who nurtured me, a stranger, in their image, during difficult times in wartime Britain.

Inequality Hath No Equal

The Life and Times of Edward Samuel Layhe

Born 1796

A Historical Narrative Documentary

By

Neville Layhe née Corner

This book is my vapour trail, to be seen long after I have passed over the horizon

Contents

* Refers to bibliography - Page 111

Foreword

This is a documentary narrative about the struggle for democracy in Britain since the Norman Conquest. The shameful treatment of its proponents, which went on for hundreds of years, is exposed and embellished with the true life story of one Edward Layhe.

During the struggle, after one massacre, the judiciary closed ranks with the military establishment: 'tighter than a cockles arse', to avoid being charged with murder and the deliberate slaughter of enclosed prisoners.

Could it happen again years later? Yes, and it did. Some of the protesters had bullets in their backs as they tried to flee the field.

Chapter One

Origin of 'Layhe' in Worksop

"Layhe, how are you spelling that, and where does it come from? Ireland?"

How often has it been said to me with tedious fervour, and no doubt to the whole of the Layhe clan, "Layhe, how do you spell that – how unusual; is it Irish?" I have always treated this as a rhetorical question requiring no answer other than a primitive grunt, mainly because I don't know the correct answer.

A search of Irish census records is difficult because many were destroyed in the violence of the 1922 uprising. A search of the remaining records for the name Layhe proved fruitless. There is also a suggestion that those who left Ireland changed their name to Layhe from (for example) Lahey, to avoid being stigmatised as Irish. This is a mystery to me, as why should they want to do this, when the gentle and beguiling Irish accent is a dead giveaway?

A search of numerous US census (and other records) shows several immigrants with the name Layhe were recorded on arrivals lists as 'coming from Ireland' in the 19th century from **1860** onwards, which tends to show that there was a sizeable population of Layhe's in Ireland, some of whom departed possibly as a result of the so-called 'potato famine' of **1845 - 1852**. It also seems possible that they were not completing the census forms for some reason, illiteracy or possibly political anger, or practical impossibilities, like no decent postal service. The only other explanation is that they may have sailed from Liverpool to Dublin to catch one of the emigration boats (of which there were many) going to New York.

UK census records from **1841** showed that Worksop at that time had become a major ancestral home of the Layhe pedigree spreading out to Lancashire, Monmouth, Yorkshire, Scotland, and Cornwall; eventually on to English speaking locations globally. Whoever went from Ireland to Worksop is unknown, if indeed that did happen. Perhaps, with intellectual intelligence of making popular Irish beers, they were seeking out Worksop Priory's famous liquorice gardens; tended with intense fervour and reverence by the monks, who may have been exporting liquorice root to Ireland for beer making.

Liquorice plant and root

John Harrison's survey of Worksop in 1636 states:

"I cannot here omit that thing wherein this town of Worksop excels all others within this realm and most noted for: I mean the store of liquorish that grows there and that of the best."

He lists seven tenants who have liquorice gardens. It was well known by drinkers of fine ale, (Edward was apparently one) that Worksop was a hive of activity for 'Malting', (a precursor to beer-making). Malting had been the most important trade in the town since medieval times, as the local soil is excellent for growing barley. John Holland wrote in his 'History of Worksop' in 1826:

'There are a great number of malt kilns standing about in every direction.'

Indeed there exists today a Wetherspoon's pub in Worksop called 'The Liquorice Gardens'.

The Liquorice Gardens

(photo credit: © J D Wetherspoon Plc)

So, we may have the root of the humble liquorice plant to blame for Edward Layhe's final dénouement, with the Layhes' using Liverpool as a stepping stone from Ireland in the pursuit of the 'liquorice mines' of Worksop in the 1600s.

In the 10 year 'UK censuses' for 70 years from **1841** to **1911**, there are 205 entries for 'Layhe' in the Worksop area and only 123 elsewhere in the UK; most of the latter are towards the end of the seventy year period. Therefore there is no doubt that in the United Kingdom 'Worksop' in Nottinghamshire was a hotbed of 18th century 'Layhe' DNA in the United Kingdom, (including Ireland) with perhaps some of the literate Irish branch having departed for America in the 1860s (according to passenger lists of the period). The 1861 census of England and Wales shows that William Henry Layhe, **(born in Worksop in 1839)** was residing in **Rainhill, Lancashire** in **1861** (as a coachman to the Baxter family). He seems to have been the origin of the sizeable Lancashire branch of the Layhe family.

From small beginnings, the Layhes' have gone from being locally rare ubiquities in the sparse UK population of the 18th century to worldwide ubiquitous rarities, in the 20th century.

They are on every continent

They make surprise appearances worldwide, like molehills popping up everywhere in farmers' fields, miles from the original manor.*

With regard to the unusual spelling, (according to the experts) the name is derived from the name for an open space in a forest setting or a low lying meadow; variously known as a Lee or Leigh or even Leah in pre 7th century-old English. So it was possibly an English or Irish location name when surnames became mandatory, enabling William the Conqueror's collection of poll and land taxes.

One of the surviving versions of a meadow dweller appears to be Layhe, along with Leigh, Lee, Lea, Ley, Lay, Laye, and other scrabbly combinations of letters, not forgetting the possibility that it could have a vastly different origin and be an anglicised version of a Gaelic pronunciation from Ireland or Scotland.

With such an uncommon name there is a high probability that the bloodline is linked wherever the name is found on the globe. Wherever I see the name Layhe (on an American census form for example) I feel that we must be related and a sympathetic affinity develops.

Fireman George Layhe

For example, the unfortunate firefighter George Layhe who died in the Boston molasses tank collapse* on January 15ᵗʰ 1919 (aged 38) could have been the son of one of those Irish immigrant families. The negligent owners of the business were later exonerated in a monstrously contrived verdict, even though they were told that the tank was making 'creaking noises' and about to collapse many weeks before the tragedy.

The Layhe pedigree worldwide may well be a unique occurrence; perhaps an interesting scientific opportunity for a program of DNA tracing research students.

In Tasmania (for example) in the Bass Division in the north-west of the island, there are three or four Layhes on the electoral roll. They are quite possibly related, but several light-years away on the family tree.

Chapter Two

A Judiciary for the Aristocracy
Run by the Aristocracy

Mary and William Layhe's son Edward was born in 1796, joining his elder brother John, their firstborn son.

John, having been baptised like everyone else in this family, (except Mary herself), at 'Our Lady and St. Cuthbert's C of E Priory' in Worksop, on 9th February **1794**. (Mary was 29 and William would have been 32.) He joined the Unitarian ministry and became The Reverent John Layhe (see appendix B). A rare and compassionate missionary for the poor, totally committed to championing (under the umbrella of the Unitarian Church) the cause of the famished, non-voting majority.

Cross St. Unitarian Chapel

He operated in Liverpool, London and Cross Street Chapel, Manchester, writing his own dissertations and being accoladed by established writers on the missions' objectives (Elizabeth Gaskell and Mary Barton books). He lived until about **1855**, dying at the age of 65 and buried at 'Our Lady and St. Cuthbert's' in Worksop.

Mary's second child was our Edward, baptised on 18th December **1796** when Mary was 31. By contrast, Edwards's later career and lifestyle were totally at odds with that of his almost saintly brother John. Edward survived against the odds until manhood; a manhood that was awash with trials, pain, and tribulation, which would have tested the strength of character of the toughest polar explorer.

The next public record of note concerning the Layhe family is in the archived records of the Nottingham Quarter Sessions of 21st August 1822 at Retford (see chapter four). The Quarter Sessions happen where so-called 'petty' crimes like theft of a pocket-handkerchief (called felonies in popular parlance of the day) and their punishments were recorded.

Court of the day

One would think that a petty crime would attract a petty punishment – not so. The punishments were so harsh that if they had been enacted between two warring states in modern times the perpetrators would have been taken before a war crimes tribunal and would not have seen the light of day for a very long time.

Stocks

Floggings and hours in the stocks were common. Victims in the pillory could lose their eyesight, unable to dodge the array of hard vegetables being hurled at them. Public hanging for a minor felony was frequent.

One can only conclude that in those days the Judiciary was run by the 'aristocracy for the aristocracy' and, for no good reason. Quite understandable, given the feeling of helplessness and loss of control which the 'haves' must have been experiencing. Nevertheless, this arrangement of the aristocracy running the justice system was (and to some still is) the ultimate unproclaimed vested interest. In those days did they use it to their advantage? – Yes!

The income gap between the 'haves' and the 'have nots' became so wide that desperation spawned an endemic redistribution of wealth by criminal means. The plutocracy spawned in 1066 was reaping the inevitable backlash. 'Get bread or be dead' was uppermost in the minds of the lower echelons of a society that had more layers than the 'Lasagne Verdi' they never saw.

Sir Robert Peel 1788 - 1850

With no organised national police force to stop it (until the inception of the national police force known initially as 'The Peelers' in **1829** by Sir Robert Peel BSc.,) the aristocracy were losing goods and chattels as fast as a field of grain before a tsunami of locusts. Sir Robert Peel, ex grammar school, ex industrialist and future prime minister (on two occasions) was like the god Janus, facing both ways and with enormous wisdom. On one side he was instrumental in repealing the Corn Laws and improving the lot of the poor. On the other side he improved the lot of the wealthy by setting up the police force, (a lasting public asset) although they probably were not too pleased when he swapped trade tariffs for income tax increases.

Academia comes to the rescue of the poor in many guises.

As a result of these feelings of helplessness, the punishments were well over the top, by any method of measurement. It would seem that the severity of the punishment was inversely proportional to the chances of being caught – low chance of being caught equals an extremely high penalty, unlike today where a higher chance of being caught (so they say) equates to softer sentences (sometimes too soft methinks).

The general feeling amongst the aristocracy was that all criminals were uneducated scum from an inferior race and could be disposed of, melted down or incinerated without retribution on judgement day. Many of the guilty were well-educated intellectuals; locksmiths, embezzlers, forgers, shop keepers, and thoroughly middle-class individuals.

The 4th Duke of Newcastle

One particular highly acclaimed aristocrat (who figured uppermost in the sorry demise of Edward Layhe) was the IV Duke of Newcastle, Henry Pelham. Which of the two Newcastles was he the Duke of? Originally for Dukes I, II and III the title related to Newcastle on Tyne, which is hundreds of miles away from the acquisitive Edward Layhe. But the Duke of Newcastle on Tyne had no male heir, so Henry Pelham (who was well connected to King George II) was awarded the Dukedoms of Newcastle on Tyne and Newcastle under Lyne (spelt with an 'N' in those days). So (in effect) in 1756 the two Newcastles were 'twinned'. Perhaps he should have been called the 'Duke of Newcastles'. These days there might have been a sign outside each Newcastle saying 'Twinned with Newcastle'; not as jolly as being twinned with Avignon in France.

George II 1683 To 1760

This act of King George II was a pre-emptive strike to preserve the title, because the real Duke of Newcastle on Tyne had no male heir and Georgie did not want the title 'Duke of Newcastle' to wither yet again. So this is how that political right-wing tiger the IV Duke of Newcastle(s) came within easy walking range of 'Edward-sticky-fingered Layhe'; much to the disadvantage of Edward who was about to suffer monstrous and degrading life-changing experiences.

Fate moves like a ghost through our 'rough spun hessian' of lives, but perhaps it was inevitable that Edward would self-harm by contact with one of the many favoured lords and ladies of the day. Given the penury and sub-serfdom lifestyle of 95% of the socially deprived population, governed by the 'haves' at the expense of the 'have nots', is it any wonder that Edward felt the need to equate gainful employment, to gainfully setting free goods and property from their wealthy owners, thus supplementing the family income and putting food on the table; this whilst feeding his appetite for ale which surfaced again, much later in a distant land…

These were 'pre-male' suffrage days, where only Landowners like Charlie could be Members of Parliament and also vote as constituency voters, for policies that enhanced their already advantageous and extravagant lifestyle. Plutocracy perpetuates plutocracy by manipulating the laws of land possession and the laws governing voting rights, choking the very last breath out of organised resistance. Inequality such as this breeds more inequality faster than a thousand rabbits on Viagra. Slavery was endemic and the emancipation of the common man in the UK (with not one square inch of this bountiful country to his name, not one full stop on any land title deed) was light-years away in the pageant of human sentiment.

The emancipation of duteous and compliant wives was even further away – beyond the outermost boundaries of the universe, existing in barely one molecule of thought between the combined minds of Charlie and Georgie. The voluntary redistribution of wealth, away from castles and mansion houses towards improving the lives of those living in hovels and turf cottages must have been a dizzying anathema to these opera-going customers of powdered wig manufacturers, who employed labourers on a sub-microscopic fraction of a penny per hour; nearly the same level as slaves.

Not for the lowly would there be 25 paid holidays per year and 8 paid bank holidays (with time and a half at weekends) plus sick pay after a night on the ale.

And yet these same Englishmen's blood and guts were being wilfully and painfully disgorged in foreign lands to perpetuate the military reputation of the leaders of a land with little (or no) mercy for the massive squalor and woefully inadequate and pathetic infrastructure in its own home territory. The masters of inequality ruled with brutality, indifferent to the suffering that they were causing across the land.

At this time the aristocracy, living in the penumbra of the French Revolution during the **1790**s, were shivering with fear. Suppression without mercy, execution without pity and due cause, swiftly and without compassion, was the name of the game.

The Corn Laws' Effect

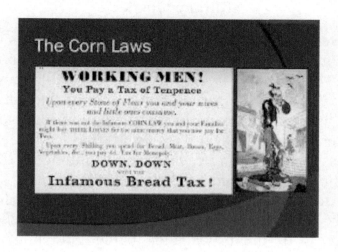

In 1815, just when Edward and the rest of the poverty-struck thought that life could not get any worse, the landed gentry noticed that grain imports were pushing down grain prices; consequently their huge profits were suffering. So naturally, using their parliamentary powers (in a parliament devoid of common man representation) they devised taxes and duties on imported grain, thus increasing the price of bread, the main component of the 'PROLETARII' diet. It was a triumph of capitalism over socialism on an enormous scale, legalised theft, and it had lasting consequences. Such was the stranglehold the aristocracy had on the windpipe of the famished and sickly non-voting population that the 'Corn Laws' lasted for another 31 years. And just like the Roman 'PROLETARII', the landless and asset less masses merely existed to produce children who would populate distant 'conquered' lands by 'fair means or foul' in this gentry dominated dynasty.

Chapter Three

Military 'Justice'!

The Peterloo massacre* was fertilised centuries ago in 1066, conceived decades ago, and eventually born on 16th August 1819, when 14 victims (and a constable in a crowd of some 70,000 souls participating in a non-violent protest aimed at reforming parliamentary representation and repealing the Corn Laws) were airbrushed into oblivion by merciless, sabre bearing cavalrymen of the noble Cheshire Yeomanry. Others died of their wounds later. A surgeon refused to treat at least one victim because he refused to renounce the protests and others lost their jobs, such was the success of the propaganda being put about by the wealthy ruling classes.

The 'Peterloo' Massacre 1819 (as depicted)

The event occurred at St. Peter's Field in Manchester (close to where the GMex Centre is now) and was to be named the 'Peterloo Massacre' in an ironic reference to the battle of Waterloo which had occurred four years earlier.

One exit from the field was blocked by the 15th Hussars on horseback, the main exit obstructed by the '88 Regiment of Foot', standing threateningly with fixed bayonets. One officer of the Hussars saw this but the yeomen ignored him when he told them to desist because people could not get away.

They were trapped and murdered in the name of law and order in a DEED WHICH WAS A DASTARDLY WAR CRIME ENACTED IN PEACETIME NO LESS. The dead included a two year old boy and a pregnant woman. Those who were not sabred were trampled to death, either by horses or the stampeding, panicking crowd.

In addition, to underline the irrational fears of the panicking establishment, held in reserve along back streets nearby were:

600 men of the 15th Hussars

Several hundred infantrymen

A Royal Horse Artillery unit (with two six-pounder guns)

400 men of the Cheshire Yeomanry

400 special constables

120 cavalrymen of the Manchester and Salford Yeomanry

Who were they expecting to face? – Napoleon on the rampage again!

Charges against some of the yeomanry were made but they were acquitted and praised by the government who immediately clamped down on freedom of speech and the press. Some of the more courageous and verbal who went into print criticising Prince George (soon to be George IV) for lavishing praise on the perpetrators of the cowardly attack were imprisoned. Nobility was not going to emerge naked whilst hypocrisy ruled.

William Hulton 1787 to 1864

That the perpetrators should go free is not surprising, considering the chief instigator of the mayhem and murder was one William Hulton* landowner, Lancashire High Sheriff and Chairman of the Lancashire and Cheshire magistrates.

This was the same judge who sentenced fourteen Luddites to death for performing arson at a mill in 1813. He was a well-known committed and merciless establishment hero who was now (from a house overlooking the killing field) witnessing with relish and great satisfaction, the screams and the bloodshed. The 'plebs', as he knew them, were now back in their rightful and lowly slot in his class conscious universe. This must have given him enormous satisfaction, winning lasting praise from his bewigged peers feasting themselves in their imperial mansions.

Unsurprisingly, the establishment in the form of the Judiciary, led by our hero Hulton, and the military, conspired, compared notes, and confirmed which lies to tell; closing ranks tighter than a cockle's arse.

It beggars belief that 20 years later an unknown number (but some say at least 60) of Chartists were shot dead by the sponsored military.

As unrelenting poverty stalked the cold and sickly houses of the poor, social unrest was brewing for decades before and after Peterloo. The opponents of giving the common man the vote made weak excuses like, "They are uneducated, even illiterate out in the sticks. They won't understand what they are voting for." The truth is that the poor could not afford to get educated, whilst the nobility enacted policies to keep education expensive; so only they could afford to access it.

Within this fertile soil for revolution was born one of the earliest organised 'anti-government' movements, which spread like a religion across the land. The members called themselves 'The Chartists' after their (as yet unrequited) 'Peoples' Charter, which listed the six reforms they wanted to see, aiming to increase democracy, thus decreasing autocracy. These were:

1 – A vote for every man of twenty-one years of age or above and of sound mind. (Women's rights steadfastly ignored of course!)

2 – The secret ballot to protect the elector in the exercise of his vote.

3 – No property qualification necessary for Members of Parliament in order to allow the constituencies to return the man of their choice.

4 – Payment of Members, enabling tradesmen, working men, or other persons of modest means to leave or interrupt their livelihood to attend to the interests of the nation.

5 – Equal constituencies, securing the same amount of representation for the same number of electors, instead of allowing less populous constituencies to have as much or more weight than larger ones.

6 – Annual Parliamentary elections.

To make matters worse weak trade unionism was getting the brush off by employers and the law. Consequently, an unstoppable head of steam was building up across the land, fueled by local Chartist leaders, like Newport Mayor John Frost in South Wales. He, after years of seeing three petitions fail when presented to a Parliament of only titular MPs, and the failed electoral Reform Act of 1832, favoured violence instead of peaceful persuasion.

His popularity (and that of his many lieutenants) was rising month by frustrating month; whereas the popularity of his peaceful petition leaders was rapidly waning. Matters were on an unstoppable path to self-destruction for the desperate, impatient but ambitious militants.

South Wales, having at least 50 Chartist lodges was a hotbed for Chartists, so it is hardly surprising that Newport, a large industrialised town in the region should be the target of their frustration and anger, particularly as it had a resident military presence in a large hotel.

Accordingly, on November 4th, 1839, an alleged 20,000 men, some with guns, (muttering how they were going take the lands off the wealthy in the whole of South Wales) marched on Newport.

The Riot Act was read to an alleged 20,000 protesters, led by Newport Mayor John Frost. But a few words read from a piece of paper were not going to stop this tsunami of pent-up passion aimed at improving the quality of life of commoners forever. Standing firm, they split into groups, threw stones and were summarily shot; the killers being protected from natural justice by the 'Riot Act' designed by a parliament of the wealthy in fear of armed rebellion.

The rioters also found out where the soldiers were hiding and promptly fired on the Westgate Hotel in which they were housed and lying in wait, having been forewarned that trouble was heading their way. Fire was returned and many civilians, (possibly unarmed ones) died in agony with surgeons (as at Peterloo) allowing them to bleed to death, possibly fearing reprisals from their wealthy fee-paying clients, the nobility, judges, barristers, lawyers, MPs, Police chiefs, etc. The NHS system existing in the next galaxy for all practical purposes.

The protesters were pursued mercilessly, being shot at as they fled and again when they were down and asking for mercy. One protester's body was riddled with ball. Dead Chartists were scooped up quickly and buried in the middle of the night, in secret within St. Woolos churchyard, with no relatives being informed.

The peak of the gunfire was said to last for only 15 minutes; the Chartists then giving up and fleeing in all directions from the murderous scene. John Frost was wounded but escaped with his life. A £20 reward was put on his and his lieutenant's heads.

Order was restored eventually and then began the trials. Some were tried for treason, having been merely asking for rights we could not imagine being without. The sentence for each was 'Hang, Drawn and Quartered'; the pieces then dispersed to the four quarters of the compass. This was later commuted to transportation to Australia for life.

Many more were imprisoned and transported to Australia.

Throughout all this, the established Church, that other pillar of society, with its secretive Latin jargon sided publicly against the Chartists for many a long year thereafter.

The period 1819 to 1843 was a particularly fertile time for riots, especially in Wales where survival must have been particularly difficult. We have the Merthyr Tydfil Riot of 1831, the Rebecca Riots of 1839 to 1843 and in 1842, another martyr 'Josiah Heapy' was created at the Burslem Riot, when the military once again fired on Chartists, protesting about cuts in wages and lack of any progress on The People's Charter.

Fifty four others were transported including 2 potters and 19 miners.

Over the next ten years Chartism slowly faded in strength and notoriety after the 1839 pinnacle of pain, but their aims and objectives came peaceably to fruition after a third failed petition of 1848 by Feargus O'Connor, and two successful Reform Acts in 1867 and 1884. By 1919 five of their demands had been met. The sixth one about having elections annually did not get through, some would agree quite rightly too!

Of all the riots about political reform, the riot at Newtown was probably the one that had the greatest influence on the speed and direction of reform. It is also the one with the least public awareness of its existence and the suffering of all those who dared to fight for our right to one secret vote, to become paid MPs, irrespective of perceived social status, and to vote regularly.

Religion continued to be embellished by nonconformist groups like the Methodists and the United Reform Church, patronised by Edward's brother, John Layhe. They grew in strength and number as healing tissue formed slowly over a scar that one day would become a forgotten memory, as oxymoronic as the peacekeeping yeomen, paid to prevent violence (but using it mercilessly).

That other pillar of democracy **Academia** or, (in modern parlance) Science and Technology, motored on unblinkingly, looking nowhere but straight ahead to become eventually the method, the panacea, by which the country would get the masses into gainful employment, and advances in weaponry would ensure the survival of the realm until the next mass extinction – courtesy of nuclear fusion or an over-friendly asteroid.

Such was the yeomen's popularity with the 'haves' for making sure that the 'have nots' remained to have nought, and that they survived, with various rebirths for 100 years or so, even though they were once disbanded in 1917, having become at one stage a bicycle brigade.

Reincarnation in 1947 with Daimler staff cars, and eventual rise to the dizzy heights of the Queen's Own Yeomanry, ensured them immortality, entombed in a well-scrubbed but bloodstained sarcophagus.

These massacres and killings must be the pinnacle of the recurring abuse of power, executed by those in strangulating control for nigh on 900 years in a self-perpetuating plutocracy that refused to die.

Against such a blood-stained tapestry of death and wanton suffering, how can anyone in conscious awareness not use their hard-won vote at election time?

So you think that after years of suffering the painful breech delivery of democracy in the UK, with its Peterloo and Newtown massacres, they would never happen again in the 19th Millennia? Surely not.

But in the next millennia, public disorder happens every few months with the miners' picket striking in huge numbers and power workers holding public protest meetings, but nobody gets sabred to death, trampled to death by horses or panicking protesters, or shot in the back whilst running away.

Nobody loses a tooth even.

Then BANG!!! In Ireland in 1972, the military steps in and 22 protesters against internment without trial get shot, exsanguinated mercilessly and die. Once again the judiciary and the military close ranks tighter than Boris Johnson's Christmas party diary.

Bad habits die hard, passion replaces compassion and protesters die.

One marvels at the inescapable fact that, in spite of the monarchic and dictatorial system, explosively radiating poverty in every direction, like a galactic supernova, doing so little to improve the lot of the impoverished and faithful subjects, nearly every person had a Christian name stolen from every English royal household since 1066. The most common being 'William' and 'Mary', of which there appear to be two families with those names and the Layhe surname, living in Worksop at the time. Either that was the case or Mary née Bayliff was giving birth well into her sixties.

One wonders if the same penchant for royal given names was exhibited to the same extent in France. However there being 15 Louis on the chain of thrones would stunt the variety of available names and anyway, who would want to be named after a decapitated monarch? So that's an unexpected effect that the French Revolution had on the subconscious meanderings of Parisian antiroyalist parents by birthright, about to call their baby Jacques once more. The nett result of the French Revolution is that we end up fighting for Queen and country, whereas the French and other republics just fight for their country – how boring is that? (No answer wanted – rhetoric rules ok.)

By some abominable miracle, no doubt brought about by the fact that we had already had our **failed regicide**, (Charles I in January 1649), and did not fancy another, Britain did not have a revolution. The nobles' butlers never got the chance to say, "Milord – the peasants are revolting," and hearing his evocative reply, "So I have noticed, and they smell a bit too."

Unsurprisingly then, our Edward Layhe, like countless others ejected at birth into this meat grinder of a world, turned to theft as their chief means of survival.

Chapter Four

Nottingham Quarter Sessions

And so we come to the most important entry in Edward Layhe's litany of life - a record in the 'Nottingham Quarter Sessions' proceedings of him stealing off the IV Duke of Newcastle. He was convicted of stealing 'essential and critical' items from the Duke's very full collection of bedding (without which the Duke would surely die of cold).

This was probably the tip of a theft 'iceberg' for Edward, with a second recorded offence. Edward, whose father William died nine years before in **1812**, would be a major forager now, trying to feed the family and imbibe his share of the hoppy (liquorice sweetened beer of the day) in noisy taverns, filled with eye-watering smoke from scores of well-used clay pipes, and with more stolen bric-à-brac than a church jumble sale. This time he was unlucky, possibly grassed up by some servant who was being blamed (quite wrongly) for the theft....

The modern archivist to whom I am indebted wrote:

'Edward Layhe (Labourer) was tried at the Nottingham County Quarter Session on 21st January 1822, held at East Retford. Ref: C/QSM/1/39'.

In more detail his crime was:

'Stealing a counterpane of the value of one shilling, one set of bed hangings of the value of one shilling and two pairs of bed curtains of the value of one shilling. The goods and chattels of Henry Pelham, Duke of Newcastle.'

Allowance for inflation puts his 15 new pence theft at £70 in today's values. The items are of such a personal nature one can only guess that Edward was employed by the Duke's chief of staff in Clumber Hall, having daily access to the bedrooms, or just as likely the laundry and washing line in the vegetable gardens, in which he may have worked as a labourer. How was he convicted? Possibly by circumstantial evidence alone, it being enough to hang a man in those days, but possibly because he was caught red handed, a characteristic with which he had great affinity, as we may see later.

Clumber Hall (demolished)

The Duke's residence was Clumber Hall, in an area known as the Dukeries, because it contained a cluster of four ducal seats, an authoritative nest of inequality propagation. So the Hall lost 3 shillings' worth of its assets in 1821, on its 117 year slide into oblivion. Its lousy economics and disastrous fire led to demolition in 1938 and left a legacy of a mere 3800 rolling acres to grow grass and trees for the National Trust. (Yet another triumph for those equalising death duties no doubt.)

Notwithstanding all this heretofore, hereafter, and whomsoever it concerns legal malarkey, Edward's poor widowed mum found her son at the Nottingham Quarter sessions on 21st January **1822**. So Edward, the ardent recycler of other people's property, was found guilty and sentenced to 7 years 'Transportation' to a province of the biggest deserted island in the world at that time, Australia.

In truth he was lucky not to have been hanged slowly in public, by a horse and cart being driven away from under his suspended body, which was normal in a century where there were 150 capital offences, most of which were not for murder or a 'life for a life' situation.

King George III, 1738 to 1820

Whomsoever was sentenced to transportation used to go to the American Colonies but King George III had cremated that bridge by squabbling with the Pilgrim Fathers' descendants in our western empire. With astonishing and impressive skill, unseen since Rome was sacked by the Huns, Georgie and his redcoats lost the biggest, and soon to be the wealthiest slice of real estate that ever slipped through the fingers of a leader of the British aristocracy. Conducting a war with astronomic lines of supply against entrenched souls fervent with homeland preservation, (ably assisted by French opportunists) he could expect no less a fate than the ignominious defeat of arrogance by perseverance.

The universal and absolute truth that 'No vote also meant no taxation', an ancient paradigm embedded in the ventricles of democracy, seemed to have escaped his attention.

Boston Massacre March 5th 1770

Thus was the Boston Massacre* conceived and born in 1768 when 5 civilians were shot at close range by 8 British Redcoats, headed by Captain Thomas Preston, in firing squad formation. They faced a gathering complaining about opportunistic and arbitrary taxes, plus duties on common goods, and lack of representation in the UK parliament. An altercation developed into the murder of five unarmed protesters, with six wounded. Captain Preston was found not guilty and given £200 compensation for 'troubles he had endured during the incident'. Two Redcoats were sentenced to death then reprieved on appeal and had an 'M' for manslaughter branded onto their palms; the remainder were freed.

That this could happen again at the Peterloo Massacre for exactly the same reasons – 'no vote – no taxation' – some 47 years later is astonishing and symptomatic of rampant idiopathic misrule.

Blinded by pretentious pomposity, Georgie remained intact politically and died in 1820, nearly two years before our artful dodger Edward Layhe was sentenced. But his loss of America as a dumping ground for recalcitrant serfs put our Edward 5000 miles further away than America, in Tasmania, a province of Australia. This being some 9500 miles away, was a distance that would make it difficult to return to his family in Worksop, or being at his mother Mary's funeral on 28th October 1844.

England's loss of America was yet another 'nail in the coffin' of Edward's ultimate fate, as was the IV Duke of Newcastle notionally relocating from Tyne side to Lyne side on the instructions of King George III.

Edward would be effectively exiled, in a foreign climate, surviving on insect infested, rancid subsistence rations and unending punishment, meted out by sadistic guards for minimal infringements, pain by the lash, back-breaking work on roads and harbours, sometimes totally pointless hours on the treadmill going nowhere. It is worth noting that the stocks and pillory (so common back home) were not used as punishments here, no doubt because the populace, being mostly convicts, would eat any available fruit and rotten vegetables thrown at them, to stave off their hunger pangs; yet another example of how circumstances alter outcomes.

In 1822 the policy of imprisoning (for trivia) everybody who could not be hanged slowly in public (because their crimes were even more trivial) led to massive overcrowding. Prisoners were even more tightly packed than airline passengers on a budget airline flight to Ibiza. Nobody in authority seemed to notice that the punishment system wasn't working, was expensive to run and was not the answer to the problems of the gentry becoming dispossessed of anything not 'super-glued' to one's person.

Chapter Five

The Hulks

Crime levels were so bad and prisons so full that the 'do good' home secretary William Eden had the bright idea of using old wooden sailing ships as 'floating prisons'. He predicted that prisoner numbers were rising at the rate of 1000 per year (probably an underestimate, judging by the number of exiles transported over the years).

Moored Prison Hulk

Thus were born 67 Hulks, or decommissioned, sometimes de-masted ships, incapable of going to sea and fitted with prison cells and shackles.

Hulk Interior

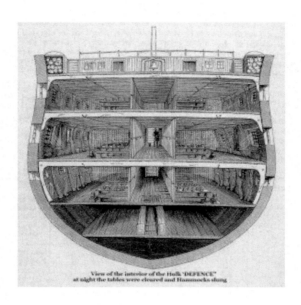

View of the interior of the Hulk 'DEFENCE'
at night the tables were cleared and Hammocks slung

They were anchored mostly on the south shore of the Thames, and one, 'The Ganymede' (a French 450 ton, 20 gun frigate (originally named Le Hébé), captured on **6/2/1809** by The Loire, whilst on route from Bordeaux to San Domingo carrying 600 barrels of flour) was to be the halfway house for Edward. It was accompanied by 'The Cumberland' and 'The Dolphin' at Chatham.

Prison hulk gaolers kept hand written extensive records on prisoner behaviour with meticulous fervour. HO 9* is a mine of information on individual records in alphabetical order and Edward has his own entry on page 39.

It states: LAYHE EDWR^D | 14 | 2ND CONVICTION. ORDERLY ——

It is written in the usual 'Round Plate' handwriting* of the day. The '14' refers to a page number somewhere else, not the years of jail sentence (7yrs). The scribe appears to be collating information from several different sources, meticulously kept, as appeared to be the practise for decades.

Such assiduous and punctilious data collection was for the mere purpose of deciding further levels of punishment or reward, perpetuating the wrongly held belief that carrot and stick, pain and punishment or loss or gain of 'indulgencies' would cause rehabilitation and deter others from criminal acts.

Against this appalling and seemingly incurable background 'The Ganymede' was pressed back into military service, and in **1813** captured a French 7 gun privateer. But its glory days were over in October **1819** when it was refitted as a prison ship or 'Hulk' at Portsmouth dockyard; a process which took only two months. Light years before the Common Market, it was moored in Chatham harbour in Kent until 1838 when it was broken up. Prison hulks were used to hold French prisoners of war, which would be quite galling for any of these in The Ganymede with Gallic pride.

Needless to say, conditions in the Hulks were worse than on shore with inadequate clothing, shoe shortages, no heating and ventilation, primitive sanitation, cholera outbreaks, mouldy, insufficient food and confinement below decks in stinking and consumptive air.

The political proponents of the scheme thought that 'Male prisoners sentenced to transportation should be put to hard labour, improving the navigation of the Thames'.

Sleeping 'arrangement' in a hulk

In one such ship, each had an average sleeping space of 5 feet, 10 inches long, by 18 inches wide. Weekly rations consisted of biscuits and pea soup, accompanied once a week by half an ox-cheek and twice a week by porridge, a lump of bread and some cheese. None of the ships had adequate quarantine facilities and there was an ongoing contamination risk caused by the flow of excrement from the sick bays.

During the early years of the hulks mortality rates of around 30% were common. Between 1776 and 1795 nearly 2000 died from a figure of almost 6000 convicts serving their sentence on board the hulks. Deceased prisoners could lie undiscovered for days. On being found they were loaded unceremoniously with others into boats, rowed ashore and buried in shallow, unmarked, mass graves on the riverside, discovered with disgust many years' later when further docks and infra structures were being built. That was town planning in a coma and at its peak of unconsciousness.

Those charged with condoning the horror were quick to point out that transferees from land jails were already sick when taken aboard, which betrays the appalling attitude of self-preservation amongst those who could activate change, but willingly neglected to do so.

Given that felons were treated so harshly it would be natural to assume that they would be deterred from re-offending or even embarking on a career which resulted in them 'borrowing' the property of others as a way of life. This was not the case however.

The Industrial Revolution Banishes Galloping Poverty

No improvement in crime rate would occur until the industrial revolution had matured and academia, the source of that revolution, had put willing hands to work in ever burgeoning manufacture, commerce and infrastructure development; this type of activity could only grow if it was led by a political will to improve Britain's balance of trade with the rest of the world.

Chapter Six

Whisperings of Change

Not everyone was afflicted with anaesthesia towards the plight of the prisoners however. John Howard, who became Sheriff of Bedfordshire, started campaigning for prison reform on a major, wide ranging scale.

John Howard FRS 1726 to 1790

He was a remarkable humanist, having earned his great wealth by inheritance. In his travels to Portugal to see the effects of the Lisbon earthquake his ship was captured by the French and he became a prisoner of war by internment (to be exchanged two months later with a French officer). His prison experience catalysed a passionate interest in prison reform. He calculated that he had travelled 42,000 miles on seven trips to the continent, and at home, doing prison inspections, finding conditions which were loathsome wherever he went. Normally Sheriffs' deputies would do the inspections, but he insisted on getting the first-hand experience for himself.

He campaigned strongly for the abolition of Jailers' Fees. Jailers were not salaried and prisoners had to pay for their food, bedding and everything they needed to survive. If they could not pay they could stay in jail!

He promoted 'single celling' for better health and hygiene, which spread to America. He did all this by travelling widely on prison inspections and personally giving evidence at House of Commons Committees. As a great philanthropist, he provided improvement to tenant's cottages on his estate, wholly out of character with the average gentry, with whom he did not mix, being a very private and some would say difficult to get on with 'individual'.

He also targeted the floating hulks which were built to last no more than two years, filling a 'temporary' gap in prison construction. The first authorisation in 1776 for their use was for only two years. Parliament would regularly renew the Act until (80 years later in 1857) their use was abandoned by not renewing the Act. This resulted in the birth of Brixton, Pentonville and Chatham prisons. The Hulks protracted lifespan was caused mainly by the prevailing opinions about punishment not being effective unless it included pain, hard labour and physical suffering as a cure for bad behaviour. This was of course, on top of confinement in a small space, sometimes solitary and certainly damp, with only rats for company. In 1790 whilst visiting a Russian prison in the Ukraine he contracted typhus and died a short while later. So he spent his wealth,

The John Howard Statue

his time and his life on championing the cause of the downtrodden, only for the filthy prisons, many of which shunned change, to take their ironic revenge on him.

One hundred years later, a bronze statue in his honour was erected in St. Paul's Square, Bedford. An honour which he always shied away from during his life.

Seventy years after John Howard's death there were still those aware of the stinking miasma of multi-faceted poverty flowing in torrents of starvation, poor education, poor health care and low income in dangerous jobs, along the tightly packed streets of new generation towns and cities. They identified the lack of progress of voting rights for everyone, with the parliamentary power of the rich being ingrained in the woodwork of the electoral boundaries which had been set by royal dictate centuries ago. Sizes of constituencies varied widely, with some as small as 100 voters, all of whom had to be land or property owners. Some could be bribed or coerced into voting for their representative e.g. the Lord of the Manor, on whom they might depend for accommodation and a livelihood.

Under the old rules a small constituency could elect a disproportionate number of MPs and gain undemocratic advantage over change in the law and finance allocation.

Championing this blockage on the route to true democracy were Prime Minister the Duke of Wellington and Prime Minister Earl Grey who fought to establish change through the medium of parliament and the introduction of a 'Reform Act' which would disrupt the existing establishment based on patronage, ancient diktats from 'divine rights kings' and vested interests in a big way.

Duke of Wellington 1769 to 1852

Charles Grey, 2nd Earl Grey 1764 to 1845

The Duke resigned as PM due to lack of support from George IV in the final stages of the 2nd attempt to pass the bill. When the monarch died in 1830 the 2nd. Earl Grey, (well out of favour with George IV) became Prime Minister in that year. He was a devout Whig politician, and completed four years of political reform that had significant and sustained impact on the development of democracy in Britain. Some credit him with the birth of democracy which had been suffering the agonies of labour for so long against a maelstrom of political intrigue and vested interests at every twist and turn of the power struggle between the plebs and the gentry.

Benjamin Disraeli KG.PC.FRS 1804 to 1881

No less a person than Prime Minister Benjamin Disraeli KG, PC, FRS, spotted the complexity and wide-ranging nature of the problem. By refusing to re-institute the Corn Laws he clashed with farmers and rich landowners', summing it up aptly in his novel 'Sybil' published in 1845 when he likened the UK population to:

'Two nations between whom there is no intercourse and no sympathy; who are ignorant of each other's habits, thoughts and feelings, as if they were dwellers in different zones or inhabitants of different planets; who are formed by different breeding, are fed by different food, are ordered by different manners, and are not governed by the same laws....the rich and the poor'.

This was social lamination on a grand scale, with two cultures within one country, one enjoying the riches and wealth flowing in cataracts around their huge estates, treating the lower with disdain, like tadpoles in a stagnant pond hidden from view by a layer of Ginny Green teeth. (Duckweed.)

Polarisation into two groups, the wealthy and the 'unworthy' was endemic and encouraged by law; life threatening and seemingly an unstoppable bindweed anchoring the masses to their hovels, empty food cupboards and fire grates. It would seem that even a spell in prison would not entitle you to three square meals a day and a bed – unlike today!

And so the reformation of the parliamentary system rumbled on with a plethora of bills and legislation changes, white-water rafting through parliament until 'one man one vote' democracy was left floating in clear water.

However, it was not one woman one vote, fully, in the UK until 1928; old habits die hard in politics.

Prison reform and the birth of democracy came far too late however to help our Edward, languishing 9000 miles away doing his bit to secure one tent peg in a far corner of the canvas, stretching tautly over the burgeoning British Empire.

Chapter Seven

Land Grab by the Wealthy 1066

If William the Conqueror could see what he had caused by allowing his illegal immigrant lords and ladies into England without work permits in **1066**, would he be surprised at the level of crime and the total failure of the authorities to unravel Great Britain's self-perpetuating and boiling cauldron, distilling misery and pain into every sunset?

As time would tell, the French had more than enough seeds of rebellion germinating for hundreds of years in a bed of class distinction, fertilised by raging poverty and deprivation. The conquest did nothing to improve the lot of the untitled, and in fact only served to crystallise society into layers of inequality; interspersed, held together by the crumbling mortar of crime and punishment, a recipe for dispossessed chateaux and the death of a ruling class.

Henry VIII

In **1432** Henry VIII decreed that only landowners could vote in elections, and for centuries nothing changed! So a landowner with land in adjacent or distant counties could vote several times and even a woman with land could vote if she dared. But the common man had no such vote or right to run for office, resulting in pseudo democracy still found in certain regimes today.

Against this appalling background of a failing and clearly divided society came the '**Inclosures Act'** of 1773 which took away common land and gave it to the existing wealthy, (and sometimes adjacent landowners) thus denying land for sustenance from the populace.

Typical 'Before and After' Result

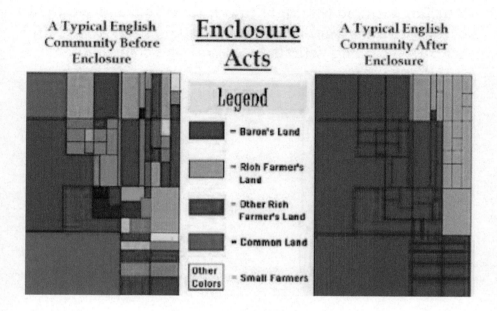

A Typical English Community Before Enclosure

Enclosure Acts

A Typical English Community After Enclosure

Legend

- = Baron's Land
- = Rich Farmer's Land
- = Other Rich Farmer's Land
- = Common Land
- Other Colors = Small Farmers

It also allowed a landowner to charge more rent because land was now in short supply. One excuse given was to improve farming efficiency. So began a long process of driving the proles off the land and into what few factories and public works were available for a meagre wage. Yes, there were petitions and objections organised, but public meetings for the purpose of furthering these were held (often in private, with only the landowners present).

Landowners sometimes bribed the committee of surveyors, solicitors and commissioners to decide many cases in their favour. Such 'agricultural gerrymandering' was welcomed by the 'haves' but it denied the 'have nots' of what little patch of Mother Earth they had a right to share with others and use to grow food, feed hens, mow hay or whatever else they pleased.

For 400 years the 'Status Quo' or 'I'm alright Jack' had been the motto of the establishment, and so it would be until full suffrage (the right to run for office and the right to vote at voting age) began to take hold after The Reform Act of 1832, along with its successors and companions.

Chapter Eight

Ash Cloud and Sulphur Dioxide

Much of this poverty driven unrest was triggered by yet another Icelandic volcanic event, this time by the **Laki** quakes and tectonic plate **separation** fissures. For eight months during the period 1783/4 the Laki volcano was emitting material and toxic gases to over 50,000 feet into the troposphere and around the globe. This was the largest emission of volcanic material in recorded history since the Eldgjá eruption in 934, even surpassing more modern events. It didn't affect budget flights on this occasion but it did interrupt solar heat gain, causing lousy weather, creating storms and floods in Europe for many years. This caused crop failure, poor yield and starvation, as the acid rain killed trees and most plants, both locally and in Europe. It was the 'summer that never came', as the Inuit folk lore said.

This effect was particularly bad in France during 1789, and added to the peasants' miserable lot. Like the English proles, the peasants had been deprived of 'privileges' such as grazing rights in an ill thought out land grab, worthy of the Imperial Rome in its heyday (one can see a pattern emerging here). The French, by now well used to eating frogs and snails (because they were free and without tax) rebelled and decided to use the 'National Razor' (euphemistically the guillotine) to shave a few heads off and to use the 'National Bath Tub' (Ducking stool) to drown the rest, and not just witches. Many of those were convicts, as well as the landed gentry, caught up in a frenzy of non-ethnic cleansing and trial by denunciation.

At its peak in 1794 the French death rate was about 100 per day. Eventually the perpetrators turned on each other, killing summarily their original leader Robespierre, in a cannibalistic fury to gain power.

NAPOLEON 1769 TO 1821

Fortunately for the French, along came 'John Wayne Napoleon', all 5 foot 6 inches of him, posing on his white horse for an artist as he did so. The English Nobility worried about England catching the rebellion syndrome. Then the 'genie' Napoleon, ended the 'Peasants Revolt' and anarchy was slain by Janus-Napoleon, the God of beginnings, choices and doorways; leading to excruciating defeat in his case, when he took on the local gang in their own manor (a downfall to be repeated in 1939 and beyond).

The English 'Administration', having attained their 'Waterloo', remained unable to improve the state of the nation and certainly unable to quell a volcano with the swords and sabres used against the defenceless souls at

Peterloo. They must have quaked, but remained glued together like hazelnuts in squirrel faeces.

Their single minded aim was maintaining the status quo at all costs and continue bandit robbing the proles by high rents plus land grabbing, taxing staple food imports, and low prices for what little was produced, alongside exorbitant rents and low wages.

Edward's rocky life path and his CV were partly ordained in the dust clouds of Laki, fomenting revolutionary forces, cementing the mind-set of the ruling class into inequality at all costs and no rescue for those unfortunates who perished. Against this back drop of national mismanagement on a colossal scale is it any wonder that Edward Layhe and millions of others turned to crime in order to survive?

Chapter Nine

After Ganymede
The Prison Ship Route

Edward spent what must have been a horrific 16 months in the rotting hulk Ganymede before being transported on the 678 ton Commodore Hayes* on 26th April 1823, which took an interminably long 112 days under Captain L. W. Moncrief; arriving at Hobart on 16th August 1823.

Hobart Town in 1821, by convict Alan Carswell

There were 219 male convicts and no females. There is a Captain's Journal of the voyage available to purchase from the State Library of New South Wales. The number of deaths on this journey seems to have been zero as all seemed to have survived the ordeal into 'white slavery'.

Conduct Records and Punishments

Edward Cook (no relation to Captain Cook of 1770 vintage I hope) was a law stationer sentenced to transportation for life from the Middlesex jail and transported on the ship 'John Barry', departing 30th April 1819 and arriving on 26th September in New South Wales after a stopover in Rio de Janeiro. Little did he know it at the time, but this law stationer was going to make it possible for the 7.4 billion people around the world (the global population of today) to read about his incarceration and that of thousands of transportees to the antipodes.

After 6 years of servitude his writing skills must have been recognised, as in 1825 he was given the task of preparing records of all convicts past, present and future in a series of 'black books' known as **Con 31** for male and **Con 41** for female prisoners. (My personal opinion is that he was a skilled forger who followed his name and 'cooked the books'.) Naturally enough he seems to have been struck with extreme shyness about committing his own behaviour record to immortality. Apart from a reference to the arrival of one 'Edward Cook' from a Middlesex jail, there is nothing to say why he was given a life sentence, or how old he was; his behaviour, the voyage, arrival details in Van Diemen's Land and Tasmania are omitted.

The name Van Diemen's Land definitely has a Dutch flavour to it, prior to annexation by the British in 1803.

Lieutenant John Bowen 1789 - 1827

At this time the Governor of Australia sent the short lived Lieutenant John Bowen to establish a small, cheap military outpost or tripwire in VDL to dissuade the French and Dutch from doing the same.

Notwithstanding that, Edward Cook and his assistants did an excellent job of cataloguing all punishable offences and offenders, (and there were many) and the punishments meted out to all the ill-fed prisoners within their ambit since 1804. One assumes that he had access to all the voluminous magistrates and Supreme Court records of the day.

In nearly every case within con 31 there are Hulk reports, and ship reports written in ancient sepia coloured ink at right-angles to the text above and also covered by that text, which in the case of Edward, makes it very difficult to decipher. This is one which was uncovered for Edward Layhe as entry no. 270 on page 90, image 144:

Transported for -   Stealing Bed Furniture

Gaol Report -   Second Conviction

Hulk Report -   Orderly

Single Man

Convicted this offence -   Stealing Bed Furniture from
                           Duke of Newcastle

7 years etc.

Here is another one for Law^{ce} (Lawrence) Lyons near to Edward Layhe's entry in the record book:

Transported for Felony

Goal Report -   In custody 8 times before

Hulk Report -   Very indifferent

Single Man

Convicted -   This offence Picking Pockets

Prosecuted by Avis a Constable Bow Street & at 235 High Holborn

Keeps a shoe makers shop – London.

Lives with his mother

Round Plate writing on a page on Con 31/1 relating to Edward Layhe.

Page in the Conduct Record of Edward Layhe

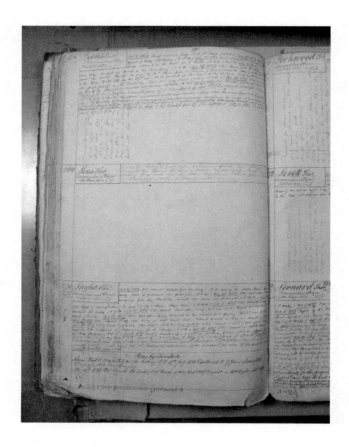

CON31/1/27 Convict surnames beginning with K (Aug 1820 - Jan 1830) and L (1808 - Jan 1830), entry 270 – Libraries Tasmania.

Layhe Edward 870	Commodore Hayes 21/7/1822 7 yrs.	
DATE	MISDEMEANOUR	PUNISHMENT
19/10/1824	Absented himself from his duty	Confinement in the Watch house after work, for two weeks
15/05/1825	Out after hours, escaping from constables	To work over hours for two weeks
18/09/1825	Stealing a bar of iron from Jason Steel	Charge dismissed
05/10/1825	Drunkenness conduct	**20 lashes**
10/10/1826	Drunk and Out after hours	Confinement in the Watch house after work, for four weeks
27/02/1827	Out after hours	Confinement in the Watch house after work, for two weeks
07/05/1827	Out after hours last Saturday	**Ordered to work in irons for 4 weeks**
10/06/1827	Disobedience of orders	Charge dismissed
09/07/1827	Drunk and disorderly out of hours	Confined to barracks and deprived of indulgences for 6 weeks
13/10/1827	Drunk on Saturday evening	**Working in irons for 14 days**
03/12/1827	Drunkenness	To work one month at Port McGarrie
14/04/1838	Time off work and disorderly Friday night	Fined 5 shillings
08/06/1829	Drunk and disorderly on the street	Fined 5 shillings
21/08/1830	Drunk and disorderly last night	Fined 5 shillings
20/11/1830	Drunk and disorderly on the street	Fined 5 shillings
13/06/1831	Drunkenness	Fined 5 shillings

12/07/1831	Stealing 59 lbs. of lead pipe value £1 at Hobart town	Committed for trial at the Supreme Court
Freed by servitude having served his original sentence of 7 yrs. plus 2 for bad behaviour		
19/07/1831	Tried for Stealing 59lbs. lead pipe	7 years transportation from July 1831
19/05/1836	Drunk	**24 Lashes**

Fully committed for trial / C. P.M (Chief Police Magistrates)

The abbreviations Pa11C, P11 and P13 are a mystery but may refer to local rulebooks or bye laws.

So Edward was released after nine years (originally seven), only to be **re-arrested for stealing 59lbs. of lead pipe and sentenced to a further seven years transportation for stealing a quantity of lead valued at a mere £25, or less, today.**

From many of the scenarios described here it would seem that Edward had access to alcohol and the freedom to be 'out after hours'. Which prison he was in is not recorded but Port Arthur, the biggest, is a possibility. It is now a huge magnet for tourists, self-immersing in the history of how not to treat human beings.

Again, 'Drunk and disorderly in the street' implies that freedom to mingle with the public was allowed, outside the Prison Barracks, possibly the barracks in Hobart or Port Arthur in Edward's case. This conclusion is also based on the fact that he was never punished for escaping from prison because it was probably an open prison with curfews. Freedom outside was allowed provided that he was back before curfew as implied by the 'Out after hours 27/2/ 1827' statement. Escaping was a problem because there was nowhere to escape to. There are grisly tales of how one who escaped with his mates managed to survive.

The fact that he drank alcohol shows that he either made it, stole it, or was receiving some as a form of payment for work. The fact that he was fined the huge amount of 5 shillings several times shows that he must have been receiving a wage, which was probably withheld for weeks at a time in order to cancel out the painful five shilling fines.

A Flogging

The punishment of flogging was very often ordered to be done by friends of the victim. It was designed to destroy prison camaraderie in a kind of psychological warfare between the authorities and the inmates. Sometimes floggings were ordered before the wounds from a previous flogging were healed, which must have been particularly excruciating. The second flogging could be for the prisoner not turning up for work because he was too ill to work because of the first flogging.

The Treadmill

Perpetual motion seemed assured, just as it was in the treadmill punishment; punishing prisoners simultaneously in powering huge corn grinding stones. The punishment of being placed in irons meant that he had to work in irons around his ankles, which must have been agonising.

Punishment for female prisoners was even more psychologically soul destroying.

The Spike Collar

There was a taboo against flogging women, so shaving heads was common, as was gagging and making them wear spiked collars as a punishment for disobedience; this was a bit harsh for the heinous crime of prostitution, their original offence in many cases.

But the 'punishment' was not all one way for these women who had been sent to force labour camps, (known as female factories) so that they could be educated on the 'value of morality'.

The 300 women at the Cascades Female Factory fed up with being poorly treated, decided that some retaliatory action was necessary. The Governor of Van Diemen's Land, Sir John Franklin and his wife visited the factory and attended a service at the chapel, with the Very Reverend William Bedford, a much-hated presence at the camp, when the women made their well-planned protest.

When Bedford had finished his speech, the 300 women turned right around, pulled up their clothes, showing their naked posteriors, which they smacked with their hands like thunderous applause.

Facing up to Reality

All acted in unison and no ringleaders could be identified. A fitting salute not bettered since then.

All of the ladies in the visiting party 'could not contain their mirth'.

On July 19th in 1838, Edward was released from jail with four others, exactly 7 years to the day after he was sentenced for the second theft of lead.

This was reported in The Cornwall Chronicle / Gazette of Saturday July 8th 1838.

On release from jail lucky convicts might land a job with local farmers and businesses, staying in Australia. Not so our Edward. Somehow, probably by working passage on a ship, he travelled back to the UK because free BMD gives his date of death as April 1864 in the parish of Retford, the same place where he was taken to court and convicted.

Open Prisons, staking a claim with 'slave labour'

In the mid-1830s only around six per cent of the 164,000 transportees to Australia were locked up. These would be the villains of society considered to be still too violent to release, or recalcitrant re-offenders. In urban locations, heavy infrastructure works like harbour walls, docks warehouses, logging and road building were being done by the labouring convicts, others were being assigned to work for free settlers and authorities around the nation.

(All of the above data on Edward was gleaned from the vestiges of freely available data left on line, the rest having been subcontracted out for digitisation by various governments and organisations.)

Norfolk Island Prison

Freedom of movement was more efficient than strict confinement. Even so, convicts were still subject to cruelties such as leg-irons, solitary confinement on bread and water, the lash and deportation to hell holes such as Norfolk Island and transfer to Port Arthur.

One of the 14 executed for mutiny

In 1834 yet another mutiny (caused by the harsh conditions) broke out at Norfolk Island. Up to 1000 lashes were meted out to individuals, sometimes in batches of 300 on part-healed scars. The uprising was ruthlessly quelled. Fourteen mutineers were eventually hanged in several batches in front of all other prisoners.

In other prisons convicts sometimes shared deplorable conditions. One convict described the working:

"We have to work from 14 to 18 hours a day, sometimes up to our knees in cold water 'til we are ready to sink with fatigue...The inhuman driver struck one, John Smith, with a heavy thong."

So there we have it – the main purpose of cruel transportation had ever been to deter French and Dutch governments from acquiring the antipodes by stealth and gradual infusion of British DNA into what was in fact an area of outstanding natural beauty, untapped mineral wealth and all of the resources required to sustain a source of wealth for the rulers of the British Empire. All of the convicted were in fact 'Political Prisoners', mere pawns, incarcerated and transported for perfidious political ends, a practise since outlawed.

Actual imprisonment was not the main aim of capture and exile. Another aim of perfidious Albion was to create a facsimile of life back home, without shackles and 'puff pastry' layers of hereditary Dukes, Marquesses, Lords, Earls, Viscounts and Barons. It would be a larder from whence future warriors could be drawn to defend the inequalities of Britain against the even larger inequalities threatened by other world powers. For all practical purposes it would become a republic within a monarchy with its own taxation and benefits system (a lesson learned the hard way).

Pest Control?

It would be a land without enclosure, without hedges and dry stone walls, without hump-backed bridges and streams, no badgers, foxes or rabbits (at least not for a while).

There would be no common land to lose except by the downtrodden indigenous population. There would be a willingness to develop open prairie culture on a massive scale when the embarrassment of convict history had melted away from the public conscience. Forbears with striped suits would become a badge of honour for the way they came through the excruciatingly hard times with life and dignity maintained.

Prairie style

Little did our Edward know that he was a microscopic tooth in a small cog, lubricated by sweat and tears, deeply buried within a huge windmill, drawing life and sustenance for centuries to come, from the southern winds, for the betterment of a mostly ungrateful hierarchy back home.

Chapter 10

Penal System Working or No?

Does the penal system work in reducing crime? This is one question amongst others, raised by this tale of prolonged misery of incredible cruelty.

Professor Bronwyn Naylor

The simple answer is no. On April 2nd 2015, Professor Bronwyn Naylor (Professor of Law at Monash University in Melbourne) said:

"The evidence is in: you can't link imprisonment to crime rates."

She was referring to relevant statistics from a multitude of countries. In Australia this statement was against a background of increasing crime and prison overcrowding; reminiscent of that in the UK and most other countries. If not now, at some time or other.

The evidence that inequality must be the source of a portion of crime is also in. It would appear from historical experience in the UK that acquisitive crime (unlike violent crimes against the person) is committed by two largely different types of individuals with somewhat different motivations namely:

- Those who **need** to steal to survive and,

- Those who want to keep up with the film stars and football professionals, as in the case of the Great Train Robbery.

Indigenous Crime Rate

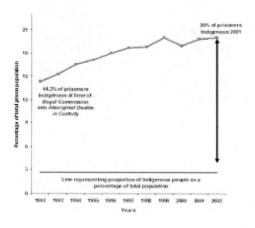

Prison populations are increasing, in spite of more judges replacing incarceration with more community service. Disturbing evidence of disproportionately increasing numbers of indigenous Australians in prison populations tends to support the unpalatable view for governments that those with less opportunity to earn a living tend to commit more crime and politicians need to commit more funds to solving the survival problems of the ethnic population. Between 1991 and 2001 the percentage of ethnic aborigines in prison populations rose from 14.3% of the prison population to 20%. It would seem nothing has changed over hundreds of years; since well before Edward began destocking his neighbours.

Reducing the need to steal to survive (by increasing earning opportunities and benefits) may reduce crime rates, however it is not a panacea for crime reduction overall. It would appear that the **inequality** and survival issues (which were cemented into the fabric of life in Edward's day) were a major cause of crime at that time. There is support for the view that inequalities are creeping back in as jobs disappear and benefits shrink into oblivion (due to world recession). Or is it caused by climate warming, benefit cuts, volcanic eruptions, strikes and industrial unrest, the previous government, the price of oil, and whatever else any government would have us believe, as long as we do not blame them?

The nett result of a class driven society is polarisation into two camps, those with flock beds and those with straw beds.

Every government in the developed world is battling with sometimes relentlessly high crime rates. Some like the USA, with perpetually high imprisonment rates, are making little if any progress in reducing crime rates. The common denominator, the driving force behind crime rates and high reoffending rates is gradually emerging to many authorities in the field as multifaceted **inequality** in all aspects of life, like job opportunities, choice of school or university, choice of affordable medical treatment and rapid recovery back to work, choice of conducive accommodation and in fact everything that many of us take as granted.

It is interesting to postulate how the massive inequalities of Edward's era came about and how they were reduced. This is because conjecture (the cousin of speculation) is always a lot more interesting than either truth or fiction.

The unification of Britain in 1066 (apparently long overdue) spawned a virtual dictatorship in which the first line of representation (the lords and lairds) was chosen by a dictator masquerading as a warrior king, who initially could set his own income from taxes by the well-known and much disliked Royal prerogative.

Magna Carta

This raises the interesting postulate that in peacetime circumstances a King in those days was merely an unelected dictator who has been chosen by birthright, rather than by ability to govern and win battles. Even the Barons felt pre-empted by the Kings' powers and thus the Magna Carta was born, putting him in no doubt about what he could <u>not</u> do with regard to taxing them, and not imprisoning without trial those he did not like (habeas corpus protection). The result was – no progress towards inequality removal and the redistribution of wealth through work. Therefore, a frustratingly stable (but thoroughly unjust) two layer society was spawned; one layer parading in silk and the other shivering in hessian.

In Britain, after several dead bodies and one divine decapitation, there was born a puppet parliament, composed of the non-elected lords; aiming, but failing to erase the dictatorial tendencies of dictator kings and themselves.

Acquisitive crime was inevitable for survival and no amount of punishment would solve the problem. It took at least 800 years (since 1066) before the remnants of the slave-master relationship dissolved, beginning when certain intellectuals said: "We must be doing something wrong". The likes of John Layhe and the Unitarian Church were constantly publicising and trying to alleviate the plight of the large proportion of the population below the poverty line. But they could do little to prevent it. It needed men of power like Benjamin Disraeli and others to push through emancipation; in addition laws to improve education standards and scope, seize job creation opportunities and phase out workhouses (which were said to be worse than jails). To spread the wealth of a prosperous nation more evenly and put more effort into rehabilitation of the growing prison population, who bore the everlasting stigma of conviction, was a lasting challenge.

After years of unsuccessful attempts by chartist 'Plug Plotters' to persuade the government by petition and local damage to the fabric of society (otherwise known as suppressed rebellion) the Reform Acts were passed with much pain and eye watering. *

They laid the groundwork for full male suffrage which took until 1918 to complete. Ten years later women received the vote on the same terms as men (over the age of 21) as a result of the **Representation of the People Act 1928**.

The Tynwald

Forty years earlier the Isle of Man government, 'The Tynwald', with its reliably tribal Celtic and Viking DNA had pre-empted the mainland government by granting women the vote, much to their credit. This was explained as being due to their apolitical system of government. No Labour leader, no Tory leader and certainly no Lib-Dem leader; all posturing for credibility when maybe they had none to start with.

However the fact that aristocrats became extinct on the island through loss of habitat may have a lot to do with it. One of them sold theirs to the Crown as part of the family silver in 1828 for £417,144 (£20 M today) and a £2000 pension (£150,000 today). The loss of 'Ducal' gaff, along with their vested interests, (banished over the horizon towards London) must have played a significant role in the islands more modern approach, making it a model democracy in a harsh and backward facing 'Grosse' Britagne.

The Welsh Assembly

Amazingly, yet another Celtic Crown territory, the Principality of Wales is blazing a path to give 16 year-olds the right to vote, yet another crusade to go with free prescriptions for all, and free parking in hospitals for staff and patients. This they have achieved since taking devolved powers, like Scotland. Why do smaller centres of government have such dashing momentum in satisfying the will of the majority, whilst the mainstream administration suffers from ponderous shackling inertia?

And so after the passage of about 800 long years, the slightly more democratic, fully emancipated system from which we enjoy/suffer today was ejected from the sceptred Anglo-Saxon womb along with:

The Magna Carta,

Dissolution of the Monasteries,

Civil War,

Regicide,

Resurrection of the Monarchy,

The Enclosures Act,

The Boston Massacre,

The American War of Independence,

The Corn Laws,

The Riot Act,

The Peterloo Massacre,

The Luddite Riots,

Abolition of Slavery,

Plug Plotters,

Universal Suffrage,

The Miners' Strike.

(Not forgetting several wars with the neighbours from hell
with great and unequalled loss of life.)

Chapter Eleven

Democracy in the Making

So what is democracy?

The Greeks managed to get full enfranchisement about 1300 years before the penny dropped in the UK and Europe.

Greek 'Parliament'

Eventually, after several attempts, the Greeks got their democracy process working for the good of all. (Interestingly, to them the word 'aristocracy' meant 'rule by the elite' whilst the word 'democracy' meant 'rule by the populace'.) So there could be an aristocracy in existence prior to one of its natural successors – a democracy or even an oligarchy – that's rule by several partners, some of whom may be more equal than others.

It is said that the super powers show symptoms of interplay between oligarchy and democracy and oligarchy and dictatorship, depending on what outcomes they wish to achieve.

Class distinction?

Other aristocracies like that of the Pharaohs went to great lengths to keep the autocracy in the family by ensuring that close relatives married the ruler; thereby perpetuating the royal dynasty and guaranteeing multiple congenital disorders for some of the progeny.

In recent European history the practice of royal dynasties excluding commoners from lineage and intermarrying other slightly related royal dynasties, ensured that some of the progeny would inherit a bit more than wealthy titles and huge tracts of terra firma, namely haemophilia.

So what are the key ingredients of a sustainable democracy that can withstand the return of either rule by aristocrats, the aforesaid 'aristocracy system', or rule by a dictator under sub martial-law conditions?

Larry Diamond, professor of Sociology and Political Science at Stanford University and a senior fellow at the Hoover Institution, (a conservative policy think tank) is a firm believer that for democracy to flourish, four key elements must co-exist, namely:

- A free and fair political system.

- The active participation of the people.

- Protection of the human rights, of all citizens.

- A rule of law, in which the laws and procedures apply equally to all citizens.

At last we are getting somewhere, and there is hope on the horizon, but wait, interestingly Larry makes no mention of religion and leaves it to float uncontrollably in a sea of superstition and bigotry, from where it can lie in wait and snipe at democracy, with deadly effect.

Religion is part of culture, and cultural activities flourish when survival problems have been solved. It can be used to successfully shape a democracy, or to bring it down. By this definition war is a part of culture, so the dangers of ignoring culture are clear. In Edward's era, only the wealthy had conquered the survival problem.

Unfortunately, they did it at the expense of the lower echelons of society, namely the impoverished poor.

The People's Poverty Trap

The proles were caught in a huge pitcher-plant flytrap from which they had no hope of escape; under an aristocratic and autocratic government bent on maintaining the status quo by dedicated self-interest and its self-believing propaganda and legislation. It was a miracle there wasn't a national revolution (as happened just a few miles away in France and eventually Russia).

For true democracy to prosper it would seem that five, (not four) separate and distinct functions of society, including **ecclesiastical control,** must coexist independently and without the power of veto over each others' conclusions, and each must have a functional head, or controlling body.

The 'Five Pillars of Democracy' (not in order of importance) are:

- **The Judiciary and Justice System**

  Lord Chief Justice

- **Academia and the Natural Sciences**

  Chief Scientific Adviser

- **Ecclesiastical Organisation**

  Archbishop

- **Military Forces**

  Chief of the Defence Staff

- **Emancipated Parliamentary Government**

  Prime Minister

(If you feel desperate to put them in order of importance then you are probably biased and not fit to govern!)

So how does it work? Surely this is a recipe for chaos. What if they disagree with each other?

<u>For democracy to succeed consensus and compromise is the key to advancement.</u>

Military Dictators

Dictatorship happens when one of these five takes charge of one or more of the others, e.g. if Military takes charge of Parliament (as in Cromwell's day), or the Church rules the Judiciary system (as in the days of the Spanish Inquisition). When this happens there can be outcomes which we know instinctively may cause more chaos and injustice than we already have, unless it is of course, in a cause aimed at creating democracy, as in Cromwell's time.

All of this is not at variance with either the Diamond or Naylor hypotheses. In Bronwyn Naylor's approach we see the pillar of Academia in which she resides, bringing public opinion and pressure to bear on the pillars of the Justice and Government systems to do something about inequality in opportunity and inequality of status.

Likewise John Layhe was standing on a different pillar, the Ecclesiastical pillar, trying to bring public opinion and pressure to bear on the same two pillars which could initiate change towards a better society.

John, (145 years ago) was championing the same cause of the poor, shouting into the dark stormy night and getting no echo; no response from the impeccably titled, hereditary, mostly male peasant bashers, hiding in their castles, behind their heraldic shields; looking suspiciously like the visage on the huge family portrait, hung over the mantelpiece, atop a blazing log fire. His and the church's efforts were a sticking plaster exercise on a gangrenous torso. They might as well have been throwing farthings into a bottomless pit, called charity.

I am indebted to Professor Diamond for catalysing my train of thought on the architectural structure of true democracy, but to myself for managing to retrofit the role of religion into a secular definition of democracy, akin to the pagan Greek model. Polytheistic gods were given the human passions of anger and frustration as society was in permanent appeasement mode, using human sacrifice and lavish grave goods. Thus ensuring drought, famine and other disasters were kept at bay; the dead would maintain status in the afterlife. No wonder monotheism, being based on compassion to and care of thy neighbour prospered in the various forms we see today, and in the Health and Safety at Work Act no less.

But beware of imitations. Pseudo democracy systems exist today in various places east of the UK, where you can vote for any candidate you like, providing the candidate has been selected for candidacy by another authority which trumps the level of authority; which means you are now casting your now useless vote, which will not necessarily bring about change in policies.

Once the five pillars of democracy are in place namely:

- A system of representative governance in financial and legislative control,

- A military function under parliamentary control,

- A basic religious system in harmony with itself and other religions,

- An impartial judicial system, operating within a framework of government controlled legislation,

- A science and technology arm, powering medical advancement, manufacturing and infrastructure development.

Continuity and stable governance can happen, but only with a leadership which uses an inclusive and consensus style. The leadership must take into account and use good intelligence from the Academic, Judicial, Ecclesiastical and Military pillars about the complexities of changing national and international pressures. Pre 19th century governance was calamitously lacking in all departments which caused dreadful social conditions to worsen, limitless suffering and unnecessary deaths to perpetuate for too long.

Increasing numbers of the UK electorate decline to vote in any type of election, be it local government or parliamentary, especially if it is raining a bit.

Was it raining on the Roundheads when they died in their thousands fighting for a more democratic parliament?

Was it raining on the Peterloo martyrs, when fourteen were hacked with sabres and trampled to death by horses when they fought for 'one man one vote'?

Was it raining in the summer of 1913 at the Epsom Derby when Emily Davison was trampled into a slow

lingering death when she tried to stop Edward VII's horse in the name of the suffragette movement?

Get voting or suffer more rhetoric!

Deep-rooted apathy kills passion, meek oblivion strangles progress, tepid indifference truncates true destiny.

Chapter Twelve

The Role of Royalty in a Democracy

How can royalty exist in the face of democracy?

Edward's Crown

Around the edifice of democracy the head of royalty soldiers on.

Having been the initiator of the massive problems of a dual-layer society since 1066, royalty was borne aloft by patriotism, buttressed by a failed regicide. This alone was evidence enough of the public's desire to have a figurehead transcending the morass of cyclic political tides, who could represent stable family life in spite of adverse political pressures.

A murmuration of starlings

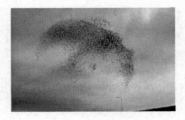

To many it is far more worthy to fight for a tangible and likeable King (or Queen) than it is to fight for a nebulous and perhaps unworthy country, ruled by a murmuration of politicians busily getting nowhere but putting on a good show for the masses.

'Thou shalt not commit adultery'

The present royal family wandered outside the Ten Commandments, giving grounds for divorce and shattering the image of everlasting tranquillity in the countries most revered family. It spawned the height of ambivalence and vacillation in many. The self-righteous sanctimonious choirs of condemnation throughout the land began to realise that human frailty was not limited to themselves, but was universal in its application and consequences.

Such protocol busting dalliances eventually endeared most royalists to a royal effigy which was even more human when wearing the cloak of sin, than it was when sporting an impeccably polished halo.

In today's liberal social atmosphere would Edward VIII have had to abdicate through wanting to marry a divorced lady-friend? I think not – considering that the second in line to the throne has also been divorced. How have times changed? (One last piece of rhetoric.)

However, at last, after a millennium of unscrupulous exploitation of the British Empire's resources (both mineral and human) the reins of power fell where they belong, into the hands of those who had suffered the most.

Inequality had not been completely conquered, but it was reduced in this country to a level at which many more were now 'more equal than they used to be'.

They could work to survive, saved from penury and disease by Academia; the one pillar of democracy that

92

could power industrial and medical advancement without fear or favour, and with universal application.

And so it was that I came to the conclusion rampant inequality has no equal in power to promote poverty, crime, rebellion, misery, early death and unimaginable suffering in a population wherever it exists in the world today.

House of Lords

No thesis on the ascent or decline (depending on your point of view) of the British governing panjandrum would be complete without a plausible explanation of the continued survival (against all the odds) of a second chamber stuffed with the ancestors of perpetrators of plutocracy perpetuation. (That was better out than in and yes, I feel much better for it.)

We owe ourselves an explanation for why those non-elected peers, (who are not actually our peers) whose forebears denied us the vote for 800 years, should be allowed to modify, nay interfere, with the elected government.

This much maligned second chamber, with its huge public relations cannon ball of depleted uranium around its neck, dragging it into a sea of suffocating tabloid newspapers, is surely the envy of our neighbourhood republics and those across the Atlantic moat; protecting us from a sabre rattling American president and his destroyers of the English language.

Round one of Donald the 'dotard' meets Kim the 'rocket man' hits your screens soon. How the biggest free republic in the universe fares against the smallest family autocracy ever, must be the best stage managed event since David met Goliath under the stage management of David.

Having decided not to slay our aristocrats, as did some of the other peasant nations, we managed to find a use for their well-educated knowledge and sagacity. In any event capitalism requires protection from the excesses of socialism and the Lords are our unrecognised shield against nationalisation of everything that cannot duck and a gradual slide towards communism!

The House of Lords (not forgetting Ladies, Baronesses, Marquesses, Duchesses, Viscountesses, Bishops and so on) is figuratively and almost literally the parent of the House of Commons. The original House of Lords dates back to the 11th century, vanquished by Cromwell and then reinstated, gave birth to a system which matured into the imperfect (but acceptable) elected House of Commons, which we now embrace.

Meanwhile, the House of Lords survived and soldiers on. Unlike the House of Commons, it is in a state of flux and could metamorphosis into being a more representative, sagacious body of non-salaried experts from the university of life, continuing to do in depth quality control on bills promoted by the house of Commons, as well as catalysing social change by producing and promoting bills out of their own stable, as they do now.

Their thorough examination of bills they receive for perusal, but not veto, introduces a ton of inertia into the system, which is said to safeguard the majority from unpalatable changes in quality of life. It would appear that they do not get involved with the devolved and limited core responsibilities of the humble and more nimble footed Welsh Assembly and the Scottish Parliament. So the Welsh enjoy free prescriptions for all, free parking at most NHS hospitals and no increase in university tuition fees, whilst we still languish in discrimination against the sick, the needy and the young - who happen to be our hopes for generating future prosperity.

We have the inertia, and the devolved provinces have the momentum, particularly towards the aims of socialistic ideals. They do not witness or suffer the moderating graphite rods, known as 'The Lords' being inserted incessantly into the atomic pile of bills and legislation changes threatening to explode and upset our canoes.

However, the devolved governments can be regarded as doing pilot trials and assuming all is well we will all benefit at some future date, whilst not having to take the risk of rolling out fault ridden changes on a country-wide scale.

The existence of the Upper House (as it is called) is still controversial to some, especially when the Lords (and Ladies) occasionally 'strongly' disagree with the outpourings of the Lower House. But this is only natural, and a healthy vital sign of our valued bicameral democracy.

Chapter Thirteen

The 8th 'Thou Shalt Not Steal'

Spectacular Incongruence

Back down to earth – have we made any progress whatsoever in how we treat those who break the eighth commandment 'Thou shalt not steal'?

Clearly we do not resort to transportation now, but was it because we did not want to do it, or was it because we were compelled not to do it? The honest answer is – because we were compelled **not** to do it.

This happened in the 1770s, (due to the American War of Independence and some 90 years later in the 1860's) by public opinion in the antipodes colony and at home. Having said that, it was true judges were reluctant to apply the death sentence for petty crimes and used transportation as a life saver until capital offences were much reduced in number, and imprisonment was the only option.

But how has crime and punishment changed since 1821 when Edward was collared? In 1821 he stole 3 shillings' worth of goods (that's 15 pence worth in UK decimal currency). A burning question is – how much would that be in today's values? 2022, after applying annual inflation over the 201 years' intervening period?

We are indebted to one 'Stephen Morley's' mathematical 'fill-in-the-box-for-idiots' method of calculation on his easy to use website. It appears that Edward's crime would have grossed him a mere £70 at today's values.

The next tantalising question is – what punishment would have been meted out, in Worksop, to a modern felon who (non-violently and quietly) stole, £70's worth of goods or more?

For an answer we are indebted to the **Worksop Guardian** which reported that from 15th August to 18th October in 2014 a shoplifter stole goods valued at £312 from four different shops and also failed to surrender to custody. He said that he did it to sell the goods in order to pay his rent (the survival motive yet again).

The answer to the next question — what was the punishment meted out for four separate crimes which grossed four and a half times more value than Edwards's crime? — tells us more about how society's attitude to crime and punishment has changed over 201 years, than it does about how the criminal's attitude to crime has changed.

Prison Gymnasium

The shoplifter was given just **6 months jail** with an adequate supply of balanced nutrition, free rent, free heating, no water rates and sewage disposal charges, no building and services repair bills, no laundry bills, free prescription charges and free clothing. In stark contrast to the fate of our Edward. Throw in the odd pool table, access to a gymnasium (to make wall climbing easier, running faster) and guaranteed release after 3 months, and you have the answer to the question - why is re-offending quite popular?

Six months jail (out after 12 weeks) was the 'horrendous' punishment for four crimes, stealing £312 of goods and failing to surrender to custody in 2016, compared to 7 years transportation for stealing the equivalent of £70 of goods, followed by a further 7 years transportation for stealing 56 lbs of lead in 1831.

How times have changed

Date	1822	2018
Value of Swag	£70	£312
Sentence	7 Years	6 Months

For stealing one quarter of the value of the goods the 1821 thief gets 14 times more jail time; without visitors and a lift home!

The Coincidence

The surname of the shoplifter was the same as that of our loser in his 1821 crime spree. Possibly he lived in the same street – oh the joy of conjecture is limitless.

Prison Population England and Wales by Gender

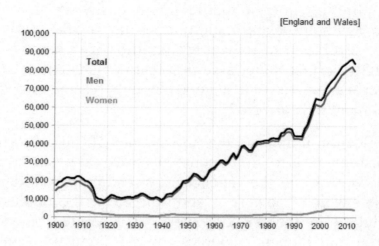

No doubt part of the reason for this apparent leniency is the same as it was in 1821 – insufficient jails, no empty spaces left on earth into which those unworthy of our mercy may be catapulted and public opinion against wretched hulks for wretched people being well established with richly catalogued precedents. (Interplanetary travel could change all that!)

Prison populations in England and Wales increased by a factor of 9 between 1940 and 2010, so imprisonment on its own is not working as well as popular belief thinks it should. Also 95% of the inmates are men. Is this because men, unlike women, are the traditional hunter gatherers, committing crimes to survive? Have we slowly moved into more impoverished times? As at 7th January 2022 the prison population is 79,056; comprising 75,900 male and

3,186 female. 47% of adults reoffend within I year of release, further proof that prison alone is not very effective in cutting crime.*

The unpalatable fact remains that punishments ranging from a lifetime in exile to a relatively cushy six months in prison (without rehabilitation) does not work. Bronwyn Naylor (Professor of Law at Melbourne City Campus) was definitely correct in her assertion that punishment does not cure crime, but is that a good enough reason to reduce punishment to near zero?

On reflection it appears that the saviour of the poor (from increasing levels of imprisonment) was catalysed almost exclusively from the science and technology pillar of society which powered and directed the Industrial Revolution in the western world. It attracted financial, material and human resources towards industry, causing massive redistribution of wealth towards those who were able to work, and were prepared to work for survival. By judicious investment, capitalists became the balm of the poor by manufacturing goods instead of poverty.

Chapter Fourteen

In the Beginning

Why would an orphan who was born 12th January 1939 and adopted by the Layhe family, be so motivated to research in depth the misfortunes of a historical unrelated felon with the same surname, born in the 18th century, who turned hard times in Worksop into purgatory and a life not worth living?

The answer is to do with mental imprinting and the need to belong. What an infant mammal (or especially an infant fledgling) sees first in recognisable and memorable form, becomes automatically and instantly the infant's protector and parent. The fledgling will follow the first thing that moves within its field of vision in the passionate belief that it is its mother.

Filial Imprint Crossing Species Barrier

Subsequently, meeting truly DNA related relatives (some 8 years later) left me a little bewildered at having missed so many precious years of bonding with them.

'Belongingness' is a fundamental human need and I certainly had it for the Layhe family. I have always wanted to remain loyal to them at all costs and this narrative is my natural contribution to their history, as if I was actually a fully pedigreed member of clan Layhe.

And so it was with the writer, who was fostered at 18 months old after sight had fully developed, but before long-term memory was functioning. Subsequently, the impressionable age of ten is not a good time to learn that your real mother died when you were 18 months old and the fact had been concealed from you.

My life story 'Room at the Bottom' explains in more detail the harrowing PTSD consequences caused by the threat of being returned to my birth father and well-intentioned stepmother.

Cliftonville Rd. Prescot

I was adopted by housewife, Ada Ellen Layhe and the late William Charles Layhe, Chief Fire Officer at BICC Prescot, who nurtured me, a stranger, in their image, during difficult times in wartime Britain. Shown is the three bed roomed semi which they purchased in 1939 for £300, where I lived for the next 16 years; initially in ignorance of my status as an orphan and an early social casualty of the war.

My adoptive mother Ada Layhe, affectionately called Tee Bee (after her father's initials) by Billy.

Ada Ellen Layhe 1904 1982

Fire Chief Billy Layhe 1909 1986

My adoptive father was known affectionately by all, including his two stepdaughters, May and Joan Lowton, as 'Billy' Layhe. I always referred to them as 'me Mam and Dad', and still do.

Marjorie Corner (Née Slater)

This is the author's birth mother, Marjorie Corner, pictured here holding his brother David (now deceased) in 1938. Sadly, she died of meningitis in 1940 at the age of 24, leaving her soldier husband (my father by birth) George Bramwell Corner, with two infants to tend. Circumstances, principally World Ward 2, made the author and his brother fugitives to fortune.

I learned eventually at the age of nine, from a spiteful 'friend', that I was fostered. He was losing an argument so he blurted out, "Anyway, your mother is not your real mother, so there".

In 1939 Marjorie lived in a humble terraced house in Princess Road, Prestwich, Manchester with George and was buried in an unmarked grave at St. Mary's Cemetery, Prestwich.

She is the one person I miss most in my life. Penicillin, (which would have saved her) was not available until many years later. I remember feeling so sad at never being able to see my real mother. It was another 11 years before I saw her photograph. From that day on I was never able to grieve again. It was as if I had used up all my tears. Nothing would ever compare with the desperate sadness and loneliness felt by this 9 year-old.

Some may wonder why I started a project about a non-blood relative. To them I say that if Edward Layhe's father William Layhe had not existed then neither would the whole of the Prescot Layhe clan. Neither would any of my children (because I would never have met their mother who was raised in the next avenue to William and Ada Layhe). Edward Layhe's father William Layhe, (born in 1745) was also William Charles Layhe's great, great, great grandfather, without whom Billy would not have existed. I have researched the Layhe family pedigree at length.

I would like to thank my sister Gina Doherty for providing valuable family background data, historical contributions concerning census records and highlighting the important role of digitising companies in preserving priceless records.

Appendix

Time line of the 17th Century William Layhe Family and Edward Layhe

Date	Event	Age of Mary	Consequence
24th Mar. 1765	**Mary Bayliff** (later spelled Bailiff) baptised		To be mother of Edward Layhe
1762	**William Layhe** born		To be father of Edward Layhe
19th Apr. 1785	William Layhe, bachelor aged 23, married Mary Bayliff, aged 20, spinster, in Worksop at St Mary's church. Witnesses Daniel Hurst and Jane Flint. Entry no. 585	20	Producing at least 5 Children
1785	Pelham – Clinton became the 4th Duke of Newcastle (Under Lyne and on Tyne)		Emancipation and social reform delayed for years by his extreme right wing bias
9th Feb. 1794	John Layhe baptised	29	Reform church gained a disciple
18th Dec. 1796	**Edward Layhe baptised**	31	Location and date of death unknown –possibly Norfolk Island as a 7 yrs. Prisoner
29th Jul. 1798	His sister Mary baptised	33	

28th May 1801	Joseph Layhe baptised	36	
4th May 1804	Charles Layhe baptised	39	Gave birth to the Lancashire branch of the Layhe family
26th Mar. 1807	His sister Mary Layhe buried aged 9 years	42	
27th Feb. 1812	His father William Layhe buried age 72 years	47	
22nd Jan. 1822	**Edward Layhe tried at Nottingham** for theft. 7 yrs. Transportation. Stole 15 shillings-worth of bed linen off the Duke of Newcastle	57	Sent to prison hulk Ganymede waiting transportation date
26th Apr. 1823	**Edward transported** on the Commodore Hayes	56	Voyage lasts 16 weeks
16th Aug. 1823	**Edward arrives at Hobart** in Tasmania	56	
13th Jan. 1826	His brother Joseph Layhe buried aged 24 years	61	
12h Jul. 1831	Stole 59 lbs. of lead pipe on release from prison	67	Prosecuted
19th Jul. 1831	Tried for stealing		**Sentenced to another 7 years transportation**
16th May 1836	Drunk		24 lashes

15th Mar. 1838	Disorderly on Saturday night		
19th Jul. 1838	Released from prison after exactly 7 years	74	http://nla.gov.au/nla.news-article65951835
28th Oct. 1844	His mother Mary Layhe dies and buried in his absence	80	At Our Lady of St. Cuthbert's in Worksop
25th Jun. 1859	The Rev. John Layhe buried aged 65 in Manchester		Unitarian missionary Manchester, Cross St. Chapel (OpenLibrary.org)
6th Jul. 1873	His brother Charles Layhe buried aged 69 years		
APRIL 1864	**EDWARD LAYHE DIED AGED 68**		**AT RETFORD NOTTINGHAM**

Appendix B

John Layhe

The life of John contrasts sharply with the life of his brother Edward.

This next section is copied from the 'Annual Reports of the Manchester Domestic Missionary Society, 1833-1908 Contents of the microfilm collection with an introduction by Dr. Edward'.

The third missionary, **John Layhe**, took up his duties in 1841 in the middle of one of the worst depressions of the whole nineteenth century. It was this depression, reaching its depths in the summer of 1842 and accompanied by strikes, Chartist demonstrations and the so-called 'Plug-Plot', which drew the attention of contemporaries to the plight of the urban poor, and gave rise to such works as 'Engels' The Condition of the Working Class in England'.

The first missionary appointed to such work. By the late 1830s the mission distributed three thousand soup tickets and provided clothing and bedding for a hundred families.

The reported conditions under which the poor existed, and incidentally furnished the wife of the secretary, Mrs. Elizabeth Gaskell, with graphic material for her novels: there are striking parallels between passages in the reports and descriptions of slum life in Mary Barton (written 1846-47, about 1842).

Layhe's reports, like those of Ashworth and Buckland before him, served to remind the rich of the conditions experienced by the poor, and provide the historian with material on how they endured depressions, strikes and then the cholera in the 1840s. But the missionaries were also concerned with a more positive outlook on life, and by 1849 the emphasis was on the creative role of education and the need for compulsory day schooling, a cause being taken up at the time by the Lancashire Public Schools Association. Denominational structure was developing with new religious rivulets appearing alongside the mainstream Anglican and Roman Catholic beliefs. Presbyterians, Methodists and Baptists, alongside a host of others, some in distant lands began to appear. Occupied with maintaining their theological corporate identities, they did little to further the cause of enfranchisement, choosing more to tackle the symptoms of autocratic tyranny, namely starvation, disease and illiteracy, rather than the root cause. Their need to avoid upsetting the government may well have been funding related.

Bibliography:

Pg.   Detail and Web links

10   Layhe immigration to US:

http://search.findmypast.co.uk/results/united-states-records-in-travel-and-migration?lastname=layhe&_page=1

12   George Layhe death - Boston molasses tank collapse:

http://www.foxnews.com/science/2016/11/28/great-molasses-flood-1919-why-this-deluge-goo-was-so-deadly.html

22   The Peterloo Massacre:

https://en.wikipedia.org/wiki/Peterloo_Massacre#Cavalry_charge

24   William Hulton:

https://kmflett.wordpress.com/2015/08/17/william-hulton-the-man-who-sent-the-yeomanry-in-at-peterloo/

35   Boston Massacre March 5th 1770:

https://www.landofthebrave.info/boston-massacre-facts.htm

39   Prison hulk gaoler's records:

http://**discovery.nationalarchives.gov.uk/details/r/C4286825#imageViewerLink**

40   Round Plate handwriting:

https://en.wikipedia.org/wiki/Round_hand

57   Convict ships Ganymede and Commodore Hayes:

http://www.hawkesbury.net.au/claimaconvict/shipDetails.php?shipId=251

76   Chartism:

https://en.wikipedia.org/wiki/Chartism

98   Weekly prison figures:

https://www.gov.uk/government/statistics/prison-population-figures-2022

The author would like to thank the following organisations and contributors for their kind permission to use the photographic images and sketches:

Professor Bronwyn Naylor

Image of Mr. George Layhe reproduced with kind permission from
The Boston Fire Historical Society.
https://bostonfirehistory.org/

KAVHA – Kingston and Arthur's Vale Historic Area – Norfolk Island

Libraries Tasmania:

- **CON31/1/27 Convict surnames beginning with K (Aug 1820 - Jan 1830) and L (1808 - Jan 1830), entry 270**

Lucy Skeet Photography
@lucyskeetphotography

Clumber Hall – Nottinghamshire History
http://www.nottshistory.org.uk/

The British Library – Hulk Interior
Shelfmark - 6057.i.7.
https://www.bl.uk/learning/timeline/item102904.html

J.D Wetherspoon Plc.

About the Author

Neville is retired and lives in Cheshire with his third wife and their son. He has 4 children.

In his younger days Neville lived in Prescot, Lancashire, now called Merseyside.

He won a schools' essay competition at the age of 14.

As a Grammar school boy he developed a love for chemistry, in which he apprenticed and eventually studied to degree level, achieving Honours.

He managed laboratories with Chance Pilkington.

In his spare time Neville enjoys chess, bridge, lake fishing, photography, poetry writing, piano playing and building Newtonian reflector telescopes.

Over the years he has been a School Governor, Parish Councillor, a Chess Congress organiser and piano player for charity events.

This is Neville's first published book. He has written a book of poems in 2 volumes, currently on his blog site:

https://www.layhe.me

I would like to thank Vicki Laskey for editing, guiding, encouraging and making possible a successful launch of my first book. (http://www.plummedianow.com)

Printed in Great Britain
by Amazon

83038761R00068